Member of the
Evangelical Christian
Publishers Association

Printed in China.
5 4 3 2 1

IT'S A BIRTHDAY TO REMEMBER

COLLEEN L. REECE
AND
JULIE REECE-DEMARCO

DayMaker
GREETING BOOKS

REMEMBERING MY ___ BIRTHDAY

A day for laughter
    friends and cheer.
A day that comes
    but once each year.

A day to sing
    A day to care.
A special time
    for all to share.

God's gift of joy
    To girls and boys,
        It's a birthday to remember!

CELEBRATING JESUS' BIRTHDAY

Jesus had many birthdays.

The Bible tells us about His first one.

His birth was celebrated more than two thousand years ago in a little town called Bethlehem. We continue to celebrate His birth each year.

CELEBRATING MY BIRTHDAY

I celebrated my_____birthday on _____(date)

In the town or city of _____

In the state or country of _____

We met at _____
(my home, Grandma's house, a friend's home, a restaurant, etc.)

PeoPle Who CaMe
WHen Jesus Was BoRn

The Bible tells us there were shepherds in the fields, keeping watch over their sheep the night Jesus was born. An angel came. He told them about Jesus' birth. The shepherds would find Him lying in a manger in Bethlehem.

Then more angels than the shepherds could count appeared. They sang, "Glory to God in the highest, and on earth peace, good will toward men."

After the angels left, the shepherds hurried to Bethlehem. They found Mary and Joseph in a stable. Baby Jesus lay in a manger, just as the angel had promised. The shepherds were so happy Jesus had come, they told everyone who would listen!

People Who Came to Help Celebrate My Birthday

Paste Photo Here

Names:

_____

_____

_____

_____

_____

_____

HOW BIRTHDAY PARTIES BEGAN

The tradition of birthday parties started in Europe many years ago. Friends and family would visit and bring good thoughts and wishes. Giving gifts brought even more good cheer.

At first, only kings were recognized as important enough to have birthday celebrations. But as time went by, children were included in birthday celebrations. The first children's birthday parties occurred in Germany and were called *Kinderfeste*.

WHAT THE PEOPLE WHO CAME TO SEE JESUS WORE

- Shepherds in those days dressed in long robes.

- They wore sandals on their feet.

- Most of the men had beards.

- They wore head coverings.

- They carried tall poles curved at the end like candy canes. The poles were called shepherds' crooks.

And it came to pass,
as the angels were gone away from them into heaven,
the shepherds said one to another,
Let us now go even unto Bethlehem,
and see this thing which is come to pass,
which the Lord hath made known unto us.
And they came with haste,
and found Mary, and Joesph,
and the babe lying in a manger.

LUKE 2:15–16

WHAT PEOPLE
WHO CAME TO SEE JESUS ATE

Since Jesus was born at night, and in a stable, Mary and Joseph wouldn't have been able to serve visitors a meal, or a birthday cake with candles. If food had been served, it would probably have included dates, honey, bread, and perhaps fish.

WHAT WE ATE AT
MY BIRTHDAY CELEBRATION

_____

_____

_____

_____

_____

_____

_____

_____

_____

_____

GARY'S BIRTHDAY

Gary sat in the backseat of the family car, looking out at the mighty Columbia River flowing beside the freeway that went west to Portland, Oregon.

Huge green trees lined the riverbank. Sun sparkled on the water and a playful breeze made whitecaps.

Gary didn't care. He wished he were home in Washington State, instead of coming back from a vacation with his family.

At first the trip had been exciting. Gary and his older sister, Loraine, liked seeing Yellowstone Park, the Grand Canyon, and many other neat places. Now he sighed. If they had left for home just one day earlier, they would have been there today: his birthday.

Gary sighed again. Mom always let him choose dinner on his birthday. He picked the same things every year: fried chicken, mashed potatoes and gravy, salad, and whipped cream banana cake. Gary's mouth watered. Remembering made him feel sad. No whipped cream banana cake this year. They were stopping at Uncle Al and Aunt Edith's for the night.

Gary forgot about his birthday when they reached Portland. Uncle Al and Aunt Edith were glad to see them. Uncle Al made his dog do a whole bunch of new tricks! Gary liked that. He also liked Aunt Edith's good dinner.

Mom and Loraine helped Aunt Edith clear the table. Gary tried not to think about not having a birthday celebration.

Suddenly everyone shouted, "Happy birthday!"

A smiling Aunt Edith set something in front of him. A cake, with the right number of candles. *A whipped cream banana cake.*

Gary's mouth fell open. "H–h–how did you know?" he stammered.

Mom hugged him. "Do you think we'd miss your birthday? We've been planning this for a long time."

Everyone laughed. Gary blew out every candle, but he didn't make a wish. He didn't have to. What he'd wished for had already come true.

DiD JeSUS HaVe a BiRTHDaY CaKe anD CanDLeS?

The Bible doesn't say how Jesus' family celebrated His birthdays, but Mary was a loving mother. She would never forget the wonderful night He was born.

When Jesus was young, cakes were often made of thin layers of flaky crust that resembled our piecrust, with dates, honey, and chopped nuts in between. Mary may have made such a cake on her Son's birthday.

There was no electricity when Jesus lived, so people lit their homes with candles. There probably were candles on His birthday—but not on His cake.

FUN FACT

The world's largest birthday cake was created in 1989
for the one hundredth birthday
of the city of Fort Payne, Alabama.
The cake weighed 128,238 pounds, 8 ounces,
and was covered with 16,209 pounds of icing!

WHAT MY BIRTHDAY CAKE LOOKED LIKE

Paste Photo Here or Write a Description

_____

_____

_____

_____

_____

_____

_____

_____

_____

_____

MoRE THAN JUST CANDLES

Candles on a birthday cake remind us that Jesus said we are to be the light of the world (Matthew 5). He told His disciples that people didn't light candles to put them under bowls. They put them on candlesticks to give light to everyone in the house.

Jesus wants us to be like candles and shine brightly so others can learn about Him.

THE BIRTHDAY SONG

The tune to the song "Happy Birthday to You" (also known as "The Birthday Song") was written in the 1890s by an American woman, Mildred Hill. Her sister Patti, who was a teacher, wrote the words, "Good morning, dear teacher, good morning to you" to fit the tune. The song caught on and was later sung in schools across the United States.

Forty years later, Patti wrote the words we sing today and fitted them to her sister's melody.

"Happy Birthday to You,
Happy Birthday to You,
Happy Birthday, Dear [name],
Happy Birthday to You."

The entire song was published in 1935 and sung (later in the 1930s) in the Broadway production of "As Thousands Cheer." It has since become the mega-classic hit of all time.

Youth comes but once in a lifetime.

HENRY WADSWORTH LONGFELLOW

*Birth may be a matter of a
moment,
but it is a unique one.*

FREDERICK LEBOYER

There was a star danced,
and under that was I born.

WILLIAM SHAKESPEARE,
Much Ado About Nothing

*And Jesus increased
in wisdom and stature,
and in favor with
God and man.*

LUKE 2:52

FUNNY BiRTHDAY SaYiNGS

*It was on my fifth birthday that
Papa put his hand on my shoulder and said,
"Remember, my son, if you ever need a helping hand,
you'll find one at the end of your arm."*

SAM LEVENSON

*A grownup is
a child with layers on.*

WOODY HARRELSON

*A happy childhood can't be cured.
Mine'll hang around my neck like a rainbow. . . .*

HORTENSE CALISHER

SOMETHING FUNNY
SOMEONE SAID ON MY BIRTHDAY

_____

_____

_____

_____

_____

_____

_____

_____

_____

_____

A VeRY SPeciaL CeLeBRation

Mr. Johnson burst into the house and smiled at his wife and daughter. "I got a job!"

His daughter, Karen, clapped her hands. "That's great, Dad!"

"I am so glad," Mom said. "I was beginning to wonder if you'd ever find one."

Karen knew how she felt. Dad had been laid off from his job just a few months after being transferred a year earlier. Times had been hard.

"One thing," Dad said. "We will have to move right away. They want me to start a week from Monday."

Mom looked surprised, but quickly said, "It's good we decided to rent instead of buying a house when we came here. I'm also glad it's summer. Karen will be able to start in her new school at the beginning of the school year."

"Where are we going?" Karen asked.

Dad named a small city about a hundred miles away.

Karen didn't reply. They had to live where Dad could get work, but she'd barely started making friends here. Now there would be another new neighborhood. Another new school. Another new church—and she'd have to start all over.

Late that night, Karen slipped from bed and went to the bathroom to get a drink of water. The door to her parents' bedroom was partway open. She didn't mean to listen, but when she heard her own name, she stopped in her tracks.

"What are we going to do about Karen's birthday?" Dad asked.

"It's coming so soon we won't know anyone well enough to have a party." Mom sounded troubled.

"That's it!" Dad sounded almost as excited as he had about his new job. "We can—" His voice dropped to a whisper.

Mom laughed and said, "What a great idea! I hope Karen likes it."

Dad laughed. "How can she help it? This will be a *very* special celebration."

Karen forgot about getting a drink and tiptoed back to her room. Moving didn't seem so bad, now that she knew Dad and Mom were planning a surprise.

. . .

By the time Karen's birthday came, the Johnsons were settled into a pretty rental house in a quiet neighborhood outside the city. It was near school and church. Karen liked going to church but wondered why people—even some of the grown-ups—stared at her. One woman said, "Oh, there's the girl who..." But when she saw Karen looking at her, she put her hand over her mouth and hurried away.

When Karen told her parents what happened, Dad grinned at Mom and said, "Don't let it bother you." Karen didn't know what to think.

After Dad got home from work on Karen's birthday, Mom told Karen to put on a good dress because they were going somewhere very special. Karen could hardly wait to see where they were going.

Dad drove them to the church and parked the car.

"My special birthday is *here?*" Karen couldn't help feeling disappointed, but she followed her parents inside.

"Surprise!" many voices called when they entered the fellowship hall.

Karen looked from face to face. Who were all these people and why were they giving her a surprise birthday party? It wasn't just her church school class, but people of all ages. "I don't understand," she said.

The minister came over to her. "Since you haven't been here long enough to get acquainted, your parents asked me to send invitations to everyone in the congregation who shares your birthday month."

Karen's mouth dropped open. "You mean, all these people were born in August, too?"

The woman who had stared at Karen earlier laughed. "I almost gave away the secret."

"It's often said strangers are simply people who haven't yet become friends," Dad put in. "I think by the time tonight's over, we are going to have a lot of brand-new friends."

Karen looked around the circle of smiling people. She looked at the pile of packages. She looked at the huge cake on the table that said, *Happy Birthday, Karen—and All of Us.* Dad had been right. It *was* a *very* special celebration.

PeOPLe WHO LOVeD JeSUS GAVe HiM GiFTS

- A little donkey gave Jesus a special gift—even before His birthday! The donkey traveled the long, dusty road from Nazareth to Bethlehem, safely carrying Jesus' mother, Mary.

- Joseph gave Jesus the best he could. When he couldn't get a room at the inn, he prepared a place in the hay for Jesus to be born.

- Mary wrapped her little Son in strips of cloth and held Him in her arms to keep Him warm.

- Joseph moved his family out of the stable and into a house. One day, richly dressed strangers called Magi, or Wise Men, came. They said a wonderful new star had appeared in the East. They had waited for the star a very long time. It was to be a sign Jesus was born.

  The Magi followed the star until they reached Bethlehem and found Jesus. They gave Him presents: gold, frankincense (sweet-smelling perfume), and myrrh, a costly ointment used in healing. But their best gift was when they bowed down before Jesus and worshiped Him.

PEOPLE WHO LOVE ME
ALSO GAVE ME GIFTS

_____

_____

_____

_____

_____

_____

_____

_____

_____

_____

FUN BIRTHDAY FACT

Close to two billion birthday cards are sent each year
in the United States alone.
This is nearly 58 percent of all cards sent.

DiD JESUS ReCeiVe GReeTinG CaRDS ON HiS BiRTHDaY?

People didn't start sending birthday cards until hundreds of years after Jesus' time. However, God sent Jesus many wonderful messages throughout His life.

One very special message came after Jesus was baptized in the Jordan River. When He went up out of the water, heaven was opened to Him. He saw the Spirit of God descending like a dove and lighting on Him. He heard a voice from heaven say, "This is my beloved Son, in whom I am well pleased" (Matthew 3:17).

PEOPLE WHO GAVE OR SENT ME
SPECIAL BIRTHDAY CARDS

_____

_____

_____

_____

_____

_____

_____

_____

_____

CURIOUS BIRTHDAY BELIEFS

- People in China serve noodles on birthdays in order to wish the honored person a long life.

- People in England who find a coin in their pieces of birthday cake are supposed to get rich.

- In many countries, people make a wish before blowing out the candles on their cake. Blowing them all out in one breath is said to guarantee the wish will come true.

JESUS' WISH

Jesus didn't blow out birthday candles, but He does have a special wish. He wants us all to love and serve Him and someday live with Him.

We can help make Jesus' wish come true by inviting Him to live in our hearts and by following His example.

MY SPECIAL BIRTHDAY WISH

_____

_____

_____

_____

_____

_____

_____

_____

_____

_____

FUN BIRTHDAY FACT

More people celebrate their birthdays
in August than in any other month (about 9 percent of all people).
The two other months when many people
have birthdays are July and September.

WHEN WAS JESUS' BIRTHDAY?

Although people today normally celebrate Jesus' birthday on December 25, we don't know for sure in which month He was born. Some believe since the shepherds were in the fields keeping watch over their sheep, it may have been in the springtime.

We can and should celebrate Jesus' coming to earth every day, not just at Christmastime.

BiRTHDaY THOUGHTS

Every child is special. Jesus said so. Luke 18:16 (NIV) tells us Jesus called the children to Him and told His disciples, "Let the little children come to me. . .for the kingdom of God belongs to such as these."

Others also recognize the importance of children:

- A Yiddish proverb states, "Each child brings his [or her] own blessing into the world."

- Writer Eda LeShan wrote, "A new baby is like the beginning of all things: wonder, hope, a dream of possibilities. . . ."

- An English proverb says, "Children are a poor man's riches."

- Native Americans say, "When you were born, you cried. And the world rejoiced."

Birthdays make us feel special, but we always need to remember: We are loved and important to God, our families, and our friends, every day—not just once each year.

People I Love Have Birthdays, Too!

One of their favorite birthday celebrations to remember is:

_____

_____

_____

_____

_____

_____

_____

_____

_____

Our birth is but a sleep and a forgetting;
    The soul that rises with us, our life's star,
Hath had elsewhere its setting,
    And cometh from afar;
Not in entire forgetfulness,
    And not in utter nakedness,
But trailing clouds of glory do we come
    From God, who is our home.

WILLIAM WORDSWORTH

WHAT MADE
JESUS' BIRTHDAY SPECIAL?

God loved everyone in the world so much He sent His Son to save them. Every man, woman, boy, and girl who asks Jesus to live in their hearts will be able to live with Him forever.

For God so loved the world,
that he gave his only begotten Son,
that whosoever believeth in him should not perish,
but have everlasting life.

JOHN 3:16

A SPECIAL BIRTHDAY MEMORY

_____

_____

_____

_____

_____

_____

_____

_____

_____

_____

MY BIRTHDAY WISH FOR YOU

That *all* your birthdays
will be ones
to remember.